THE TV WAR

Compiled by Pat Edwards and Wendy Body

Acknowledgements

We are grateful to the following for permission to reproduce copyright material:
The author, Anne Digby for 'I'm not moving', an exract from *Me, Jill Robinson and the Television Quiz* Copyright Anne Digby (pub Puffin); Heinemann Young Books for 'Fanny's Sister' from *Fanny and the Monsters* by Penelope Lively; Hodder & Stoughton Australia for 'Trefoil — Island of Tragedy' from *Young and Brave* by Mavis Thorpe Clark, (Hodder & Stoughton Australia Pty Ltd, 1984); Jonathan Cape Ltd/Author's agents for poem and illustrations 'Jimmy Jet and His TV Set' by Shel Silverstein from *Where the Sidewalk Ends* Copyright © 1974 Evil Eye Music Inc; Morrow Junior Books (A Division of William Morrow & Co, Inc) for 'John Dark and Other Homework' from *Touch-Luck Karen* by Johanna Hurwitz, Copyright © 1982 Johanna Hurwitz; Penguin Books Ltd for the poem 'Somewhere' from *Wry Rhymes for Troublesome Times* by Max Fatchen (Kestrel Books, 1983), Copyright © Max Fatchen, 1983; Scholastic-TAB Publications Ltd for 'What, no TV?' from *The TV War and Me* by Sonia Craddock, Copyright 1980 by Sonia Craddock, (pub by Scholastic-TAB Publications Ltd). Pages 38-9 were written by Bill Boyle and Steve Attmore.

We are grateful to the following for permission to reproduce photograhs: BBC Publications (Radio Times), page 28; Columbia Pictures TV, page 29; Oxford Scientific Films, page 79.

Illustrators, other than those acknowledged with each story, include Cindy Hunnam p.37; Amanda Hall pp.38-9; Maria Yeap p.51; Linda Forss pp.52-3; Elizabeth Alger pp.54-5; Rebecca Pannell pp.70-3; Sally Rogers pp.80-1; Lisa Herriman pp.95-6.

Contents

WHAT NO TV?

I was in my room getting some Kleenex for my runny nose when the screaming started. It was 5:30 on a Friday afternoon in October, and outside it was raining. I knew it was exactly 5:30 because *Planet of Death* was just starting on TV and the cartoons had just finished.

If it had only been my five-year-old brother Benjy screaming I wouldn't have taken any notice, because he screams and yells all the time. But Peter, who is eleven, was screaming even louder, and that was a shock.

I sort of fell into the living room in my rush to see what was happening. "What's going on?" I shouted into the din.

Nobody took any notice.

Mum was standing in front of the TV, her arms folded in front of her. She was dripping wet all over, from her yellow rain hat down to her black rubber boots. Peter was jumping up and down yelling at her, and Benjy was lying on the floor rolling and kicking and screaming.

And then I saw what had happened — Mum had turned off the TV!

"Hey!" I ran and grabbed her arm. "You can't do that. We've just started to watch *Planet of Death*."

"You're getting wet," she said, looking down at her dripping raincoat.

"*Mum!*" What was the matter with her? "*Didn't you hear me?* We were watching that!"

She looked me in the eye. "You are not watching any more television," she said calmly.

"What? What are you talking about?"

"She means it, Anne." Peter gave the coffee table a swift kick. "She really means it."

"*What?*"

Mum started to take off her coat. It had dripped all over the carpet. "I'm soaking," she said. "I'm going to change. We'll talk about it later." And she disappeared down the basement stairs.

"Is she nuts or something?" I still didn't understand what was going on, but I wasn't about to let it get me. She'd had a lot of strange ideas lately. I switched on the TV and started to mop up the wet patches on the rug with some Kleenex. It's fantastic! I could just imagine what she'd do to us if *we* dripped all over the carpet.

"It's no good, Anne." Peter kicked the table again. "She's pulled out the cable. It won't work."

I turned and stared at the TV. There were black lines running across the set, and as I stared, a weird crackling noise began to grow louder.

"She's gone crazy!" I leaned over to see the back of the set. Sure enough, there was the cable that came in through a hole in the floor —just lying there.

"Ever since she started going to university she's been getting funny ideas," said Peter, and he stabbed the TV off with a grey-socked foot.

I nodded. He was right. Ever since the divorce, when Mum decided she was going back to college to train to be a teacher—ever since then she'd started to change. And not for the better.

"First it was her clothes." I sat down next to Peter on the hide-a-bed. "She used to have such pretty dresses—a new one for every party practically. And now she never wears a dress, only corduroys and T-shirts. And she never puts on any make-up or goes to get her hair done. She used to go every week."

"And she's been getting stricter and stricter." Peter started to kick the back of the hide-a-bed. "All day at school we have teachers, and now we're getting another one at home. It isn't fair. She used to let us do what we wanted."

Benjy stuck his head out from behind us. "She makes me go to bed at seven o'clock and I can't have any candy." His voice rose to a wail.

"Crybaby!" said Peter. "You're always crying."

"I'm not. I'm not always crying," Benjy cried, and he punched Peter in the stomach.

"Ow!" Peter grabbed him. "You monster!"

Benjy started to go red in the face. He was holding his breath getting ready to scream.

"Oh, let him go," I snapped. "He'll scream for Mum and then we'll be the ones in trouble."

"Okay for you," snarled Peter, releasing his grip on Benjy's red sweater. "He didn't punch you."

"All I know," I said as Benjy scuttled away, "is that we're missing *Planet of Death* just because of some cracked idea of Mum's. Why doesn't she want us to watch it?"

Peter shrugged. "She just marched in and turned it off. When I tried to turn it on again she yanked out the cable. Maybe we're broke. Maybe she's going to sell it!"

I thought about that. He could be right. When Mum was still married to Dad we used to have a lot of money. At least we lived in a big house—and even had two TVs, one in colour. But when Mum and Dad got divorced they sold the house and the colour TV and the cars, and we moved here. Benjy and Peter have to share a bedroom and Mum sleeps on the hide-a-bed. We would have rented an apartment, only we couldn't find one that would take three kids.

Just then there was the sound of dishes rattling in the kitchen. "She's getting dinner," said Peter. "Let's go talk to her."

We all crowded into the tiny kitchen. In our old house the kitchen had been big—big enough to have all our meals in—but now we had to eat in the living room. We had the dining table pushed down to one end. I didn't mind. It was cosy, and there was a fireplace too. When winter came we could eat and watch the fire at the same time.

I didn't really mind leaving our old house. I guess it was because Mum was so unhappy there and always weeping around. I didn't even mind leaving my friends — I thought I'd make new friends here when I joined the after-school teams. But Mum makes me babysit Benjy every day after school, so I haven't had a chance to make any friends. She says our future depends on what she's doing. What good is the future when my whole life is messed up right now? But she never notices that.

Suddenly I smelled what was frying on the stove — steak! I turned and gave Peter a look, and he looked at me. No one buys steak if they've just run out of money — so why couldn't we watch TV?

"Mum," I said, "why can't we watch the TV?"

"Friday is our favourite evening," Peter chimed in. "It's *Robot Robbers* tonight."

"And two of the best game shows," I said quickly. "And a western movie."

"And I want to see the cartoons," wailed Benjy. "I want to see the cartoons. I want to see—"

"There aren't any, stupid." Peter glared at him. "That's in the morning."

"Oh! Well, I want to see them in the morning. I want to see them. I —"

I gave him a poke to shut him up. "Mum!" She was exasperating. There she stood, her wet hair wrapped up in a towel, calmly turning steak as if nothing was the matter. "Mum! Why? Why?"

"Because," she said slowly, "I have decided that watching TV is bad for you."

"Bad for us?" Peter shouted.

"Yes, bad for you. You do nothing else but watch TV every moment you get."

"Oh, yeah! Fat chance we get to watch every moment, what with homework, dishes, making our own lunches — and looking after Benjy!" I was furious. How could she be so unfair!

She shrugged. "I've been talking to some people. Too much TV watching makes children violent."

"People at the university, I bet," sneered Peter.

"Yes, as a matter of fact," Mum agreed.

"Well, shows you how much they know. We're not violent. We don't go round beating each other up."

"No. But you argue and squabble all the time," Mum said.

She was really serious. She really meant it. She really believed TV was making us violent! Me, who couldn't even kill a wasp!

"Ha!" said Peter. "How can we be violent if we're watching TV all the time like you said? We wouldn't have the time, would we? Ha!"

"Don't split hairs, Peter." Mum smiled at him. "I'm not going to discuss it any more. We are all having a complete rest from television and that's that."

Well, we relaxed a bit when she said that and sat down and ate our steak quite cheerfully. Both Peter and I thought she meant a complete rest for one night. It was a nuisance and we had a boring, boring evening. I did some math homework, which I hate, and Peter tried to make a model he'd been given for his birthday, but it broke when he was gluing it and he kicked it all over the floor. And Benjy—well, he didn't do anything except bug me till I smacked him. Then he had a tantrum and Mum had to put him to bed. It was a real peaceful, nonviolent evening without the TV! And I sure hoped Mum was noticing it. I was glad to go to bed.

The next morning I slept in late. On Saturdays I usually get up around ten, go get some cereal and watch the cartoons till lunch time. I got up at ten as usual, got my cereal and wandered into the living room.

Then I remembered! I rushed over to the set and peered behind it. The cable was still lying flat on the ground like some worn-out black snake. She hadn't fixed it!

I noticed then how quiet it was. Where was everyone? Generally when I get up on Saturdays Benjy and Peter are fighting over what channel they want. I knew Mum wouldn't be in. She goes out first thing every Saturday morning and does the grocery shopping. She's always asking us to go with her, but who wants to do a boring thing like that? When we lived in the old house we used to take the car and go to a gigantic supermarket that sold everything. Now we only live three blocks from the stores, but there's no supermarket, just lots of little shops. It's because we live in a different sort of neighbourhood, I guess. Where we lived before everyone had large houses and flat green lawns, and you had to keep your grass cut properly or people complained—and no shops were allowed. But here people even grow vegetables in front of their houses. Most of them are new immigrants and don't speak good English. The kids in my grade seven class are from all around the world—Greece, Italy, Germany, Pakistan, India, the West Indies. Mr Burdett says it's the U.N. He's always making jokes that aren't very funny.

I wandered around the house looking for someone. Peter and Benjy's bedroom was a mess—clothes and blankets and toys every-where—but no one was there. There was no one in the bathroom either. I went down to the basement, but the only thing down there was the rickety furnace making queer thumping sounds. There's no upstairs to our house, so that was it.

I looked out the kitchen window. It was still pouring rain. No one in his right mind would be outside. We're supposed to have a "peek-a-boo" view of the sea and the mountains through the kitchen window. Even if I stood on a chair and craned my neck, the farthest I could see was the dogwood tree in the back yard, and today I couldn't even see the round red seeds on that! It was all grey, grey, grey. I turned my eyes away and shivered.

Then I saw the note. It was on the fridge door. I don't know how I missed it before. *Gone shopping. Pete and Benjy are with me. Love, Mum.* That's all it said, on the back of a used envelope.

I went into the bathroom and cleaned my teeth. It was so quiet in the house it made me shiver. All I could hear was the furnace thumping, the rain falling and the traffic muffled in the distance.

I felt hot and churny inside. Why would Peter go off like that? I could see Benjy going. He was always hoping for candy. But Mum gets his sweets in the health-food store on the corner now and he doesn't like it—apricot bars and things! Poor Benjy. He's just dying for Hallowe'en.

I brushed my hair and tied it back with elastic bands. I hate my hair, but not as much as I hate my teeth! My front teeth stick out so much I look like Bugs Bunny. The orthodontist says I need braces, but Mum thinks the orthodontists are trying to make everyone look the same—same teeth, same smile. She thinks we should all be individuals. I don't see why having buck teeth makes me an individual. All the kids I know who have braces say they hate them. Well, I would just love to have some. Every day I push back on my teeth to see if they'll move a bit, but nothing very much happens. It's very disappointing.

After I'd dressed, made my bed and stowed all the dirty clothes I could find in the wash basket, I decided to try putting the cable back on the TV. That would show them. If Peter and Benjy came back and found me watching cartoons, lying on the carpet warm and cosy, while they'd been out in the pouring rain, they'd have a fit!

I pulled the set out from the wall and picked up the dead cable. It had a silver screw on the end with a wire sticking out. How was it supposed to screw in? Maybe it would give me a shock. Once I got an electric shock from an old toaster when I shoved a knife into it to try and rescue a piece of burning toast. It was like pins and needles darting all over my body. I didn't want to try that again.

It was no use. I didn't know how to put the stupid thing back. I'd have to wait for Mum. But I'd be sure to watch how she did it, just in case!

There was nothing to do — nothing! I wandered round the living room for ages. I switched the lights on and off. I even read a few pages of Mum's library book. Finally, I plunked down on the hide-a-bed by the front window and stared out. The house was so quiet I could hear the gurgling of the rain as it plinked into the down-pipes and ran out the other end. Our front yard was a tiny patch of soaked grass, and the overgrown laurel hedge that cut us off from the side-walk was bowed down and heavy with water. Across the road I could see an old black car that looked as if it came out of the Ark. The old man who owns it is forever hosing it down and waxing it, but I don't think I've ever seen him drive it.

Black, red and yellow umbrellas were bobbing past — Saturday shoppers, I guessed, hurrying to get out of the rain. A little kid in a yellow hat and coat was jumping in a deep puddle outside our rickety iron gate. He was having a whale of a time and didn't seem to care about getting soaked. It suddenly made me feel really old. I used to like jumping in puddles. Peter and I used to have splashing fights on the way home from school. I had a sudden urge to jump up and down in that puddle till the water was gone and I was soaked.

The next thing I knew I had jammed on my boots, struggled into my raincoat and was racing down the concrete path. The little kid had gone. I made one giant leap into the air and *splash!* down I came, feet flat, right into that muddy puddle!

Black sheets of spray flew everywhere and I saw the world through big black drops that dripped off my eyelashes. It was fantastic! How was I to know that someone was just walking past? It was the man who lives at the end of the block, the one who gives Mum a ride to her classes.

He stood absolutely still, dripping muddy water like a coloured shower. "Why did you do that?" he asked very quietly.

It's funny the things that flash through your head in just a second. First I wondered if he knew who I was. Maybe it would be worth running for it. Then I decided he would have seen me coming out the gate, and he knew it was Mum's house. I thought maybe I should be really apologetic and grovel a bit and try to brush the mud off his cream corduroys — but it was his stupid fault wearing light-coloured pants on a wet day. What I really wanted to do was give another giant jump and splash him all over again — and that almost made me grin. Finally I just said, "I don't know."

He was tall and thin with very curly black hair and a wobbly black umbrella that had two holes in it. His arms were full of paper bags and packages of bread — very muddy looking, soggy paper bags. I sighed.

He looked me in the eye with a blue stare. I wondered if he was a teacher. He sort of had the feel of one, the prickly stare of one.

"Aren't you going to apologise?"

"Sorry," I said, but I still wanted to jump up and down in the puddle till he was soaked. I wondered if he could read minds.

He gave me a funny look, said "Mmmm," and walked on. Or rather, slopped on. I guess a lot of the puddle was inside his shoes.

Suddenly I began to wonder if he might be the one who gave Mum all those queer ideas about TV. If I hadn't been such a coward I would have yelled after him all the swear words and curses I knew. Anyhow, he'd better not complain to Mum about the puddle. That was all I needed.

I had just changed out of my muddy boots and coat when Benjy, Peter and Mum came in, stamping and bumping parcels on the table and flinging wet things all over heating vents to dry.

"You've been a long time," I said.

"We went and had pastries and milkshakes in the Sunshine Shop." Benjy slid around the kitchen floor in his socks. "I had a chocolate—what was it, Mum?"

"Eclair."

"That's right, eclair. It was fantastic. Better than Peter's marzipan cake. And we had malted milkshakes too—but Mum had coffee."

I had a pain in my stomach from hunger and here they were in a restaurant eating without me. It wasn't fair. "Don't say fantastic! That's my word!" I growled at Benjy.

"I can say it if I want, can't I, Mum? I can say any word I want."

"If you don't shut up," I hissed in his ear, "I'll sticky-tape your mouth." I stepped down hard on his toe.

"Ow! Mum, Anne stamped on my foot!"

"Sorry," I said sweetly. "You shouldn't put your feet in the way."

"There's a cake in the bag for you, Anne." Mum gave me a look.

"What is it?"

"Eclair!" said Benjy smiling at me again. "I chose it for you, Anne. It was the biggest they had."

"I don't like eclairs," I said. "I hate them."

Benjy's face fell and his mouth trembled. "I thought you liked them."

"I bet," I taunted. "I bet you just wanted to eat another one. Greedy pig!" I really loved eclairs and Benjy knew it. I just felt mean and angry—so why did I want to pick him up and give him a hug too? I slammed out of the kitchen and threw myself down in front of the TV. "Mum! You haven't fixed the TV. You forgot to do it before you left. I want to watch the early movie."

She walked slowly into the living room. "But, Anne, didn't you understand? When I said we needed a rest from television I didn't mean for just one night."

Then what did she mean? I wondered. The whole weekend?

"I didn't mean just one night," she went on calmly. "I meant forever."

* * *

Three hours later, Peter and I were sitting in the corner down by the old furnace. We had sore throats from arguing and pleading, and red eyes from crying.

It was dirty and dusty, but we'd put down an old patchwork quilt and some cushions against the wall. It was the warmest place in the house—dark, but warm and cosy. The furnace used to be for coal, a long time ago, before it was re-done for oil. I wish it still was, then we could throw big lumps of shiny black coal into it.

The furnace man had told Mum that the old man who lived in the house before us was a real miser and never paid for his oil. That's why the tank was empty. We wondered if he had frozen to death, because he was found dead in his bed. But he was ninety-five, so I guess he probably died of oldness. They took the bed he died in away. They took everything away except a greeny-black leather trunk at the other end of the basement. The real-estate man said it was full of junk and he was going to give it to the Salvation Army. We had already tried to look inside, but it was locked.

Peter was wiping his face on the plum-coloured cushion. "Do you hate her?" he asked in a muddled, tight sort of voice.

"Yes," I said. It was true too. I did hate her. She had ruined my weekend. She was ruining my whole life.

"I wish we could go and live with Dad." Peter sniffed. "*He'd* let us watch TV all the time."

"Really?" I was a bit surprised. I mean, I hated Mum, but I never felt anything for Dad. I hardly even knew him, and I sure didn't want to go and live with him. He was okay, I guess, but he always looked through me as though I wasn't there. He was always off looking at rocks, anyway. And if I asked him anything — any little question at all — he always gave me a long, long sermon with big words and sentences you could unroll across the floor. Once I asked him why we had to clean our teeth. Sometimes I just ask questions to talk to people. But Dad started in on an hour's lecture about plaque and particles and calcium and decay — he used thousands of words I'd never heard before. All I wanted him to say was, "You'll get cavities if you don't."

"Do you *really* want to go live with Dad?"

"Well, not really I suppose." Peter sniffed again. "But it isn't fair! If I was grown up I wouldn't do a dirty thing like that. Kids don't stand a chance."

"I was busy pushing my teeth back with my fingers. It helps me think, too, helps me concentrate. "Do you mind hating Mum?" I mumbled. I always feel horrid about hating Mum, all red inside like I want to slam her. But it hurts to feel it.

"No," said Peter. "When I hate, I hate. I don't get sloppy about it." He had no imagination. He didn't see anything that wasn't stuck right in front of him.

"I'm not taking this from her anyway," I said.

"What can you do?"

"I've got a plan. Listen. On Monday, when we get to school, I'm going to go into the auditorium and have a good look at the school television. It's hooked up to a cable. I'm going to see how it's all connected and draw a sort of plan. Then when we get home we can hook up ours and *poof!*, there you are."

"Mum will have a fit!"

"She won't know. When she gets home at five we'll have it unhooked and be busy with our homework or something."

"It's not much. Just an hour." Peter frowned. "It's not what we're used to."

"It's better than nothing. Anyway if we hurry home from school we can get almost two hours."

"Benjy will tell."

"No he won't — or he'll die. I'll fix Benjy. Don't worry about him."

"It's too bad we don't know any kids who live near, or we could go to their houses," Peter sighed. "I could go to Terry's, but his dad works night shift and sleeps in the day and he's not allowed to have anyone in."

"Well, I don't know anyone. I always have to babysit Benjy, and who would want *him* in their house for more than a minute?"

"Too true, too true," agreed Peter.

"Well?"

"Well what?"

"Well, is it a good idea?"

Peter shrugged. "Give it a try."

And so I would — if Monday morning ever came.

* * *

Written by Sonia Craddock
Illustrated by Donna Gynell

22

Who invented TV?

I know what you're thinking. It was John Logie Baird. But it wasn't, you know.

Like most inventions, TV was the result of lots of experiments by several different people, each one learning from what had gone before.

In 1877, a Frenchman named Senlecq, first wrote about the idea of television. Did that make him the inventor? No, because there was no model.

In 1884, a German named P. Nipkow, built a special disc called a scanner which turned light into electronic pulses or signals. But it still wasn't television.

Finally in 1925, someone named V.K. Zworykin, invented something he called the iconoscope. He had used the idea of Nipkow's scanner to produce a machine which turned pictures into electronic signals that went out over air waves. So he's the inventor! Right? Well, not really.

You see to make a television set work we need a cathode-ray tube — the thing that turns the signals back into a picture. And that had been invented back in the early 1830s by a German scientist, F. Braun.

Take your pick. Who would you say?

PS: Why did John Logie Baird get the credit? Well, he was the man who demonstrated the first TV transmission in London, in 1925.

HOW DOES TELEVISION WORK?

All television programmes go through two stages:

Planning. People work out what's to be in the programme and discuss the best ways to do this.

Production. The programme can be

  a recorded live (as the news and weather are)

  b recorded on video tape

  c recorded on film

This is the microphone, which must be long enough to reach over to the actor or announcer. Sometimes, you'll notice people wearing small microphones clipped to their clothes as well. The sound is also changed into electronic messages and goes to the control room down another separate cable.

a live

c film

Here's the camera. Its job is to change the light from the live scene into electronic signals and send them down via cable to the control room. That's where the scanner comes into it.

b video tape

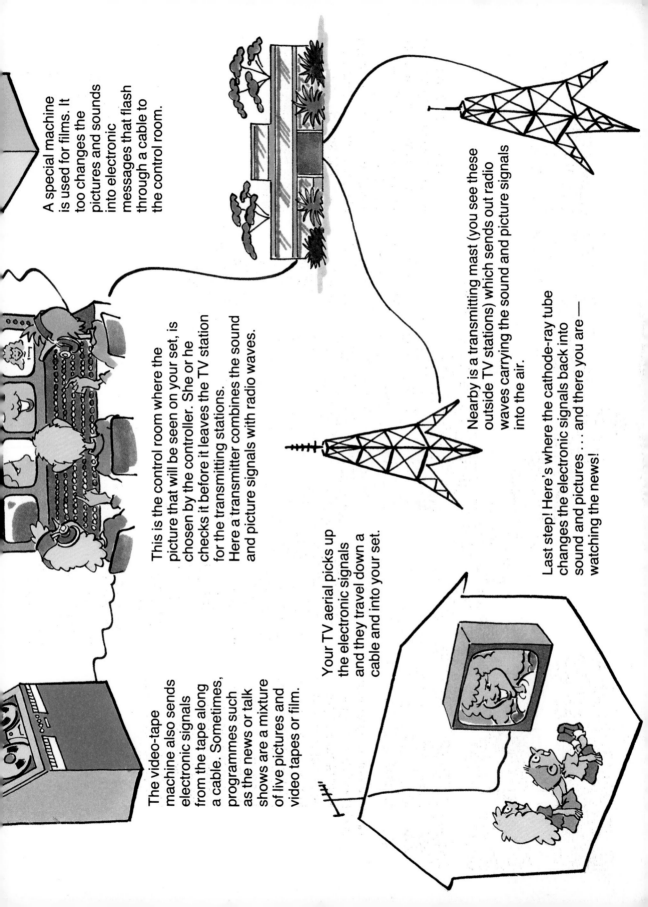

A special machine is used for films. It too changes the pictures and sounds into electronic messages that flash through a cable to the control room.

This is the control room where the picture that will be seen on your set, is chosen by the controller. She or he checks it before it leaves the TV station for the transmitting stations. Here a transmitter combines the sound and picture signals with radio waves.

The video-tape machine also sends electronic signals from the tape along a cable. Sometimes, programmes such as the news or talk shows are a mixture of live pictures and video tapes or film.

Nearby is a transmitting mast (you see these outside TV stations) which sends out radio waves carrying the sound and picture signals into the air.

Last step! Here's where the cathode-ray tube changes the electronic signals back into sound and pictures . . . and there you are — watching the news!

Your TV aerial picks up the electronic signals and they travel down a cable and into your set.

JIMMY JET AND HIS TV SET

I'll tell you the story of Jimmy Jet —
And you know what I tell you is true.
He loved to watch his TV set
Almost as much as you.

He watched all day, he watched all night
Till he grew pale and lean,
From "The Early Show" to "The Late Late Show"
And all the shows between.

He watched till his eyes were frozen wide,
And his bottom grew into his chair.
And his chin turned into a tuning dial,
And antennae grew out of his hair.

And his brains turned into TV tubes,
And his face to a TV screen.
And two knobs saying "VERT." and "HORIZ."
Grew where his ears had been.

And he grew a plug that looked like a tail
So we plugged in little Jim.
And now instead of him watching TV
We all sit around and watch him.

Shel Silverstein

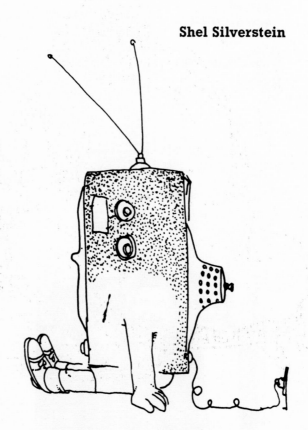

BBC 1

3.25pm
The Clothes Show
Tomorrow night is the final of *The Clothes Show Models 88* competition. **Selina Scott, Jeff Banks** and **Caryn Franklin** tell the background story from the sorting of the original 16,000 entries, the auditioning of the 400 on the shortlist, to the arrival of the 32 finalists at the Assembly Rooms in Derby. Ten-year-old **Dawn Hind** is a first-time cover girl and **Jerry Hall** gets the wet look for *The Clothes Show* magazine.
Directors GARY HUNTER, SUE LLOYD
Producer ROGER CASSTLES
BBC Pebble Mill
(The final tomorrow at 7.35pm)

3.50 Children's BBC
Andy Crane – followed by
Sebastian the Incredible Drawing Dog
with **Michael Barrymore**
The Rabbit Who Ate Paper
Devised, written and illustrated by
DAVID MYERS
Producer CHRISTOPHER PILKINGTON
(R)

4.00 Doodle
Ten, nine, eight . . .
The countdown is on for doodlers to design the latest in space travel.
Seven, six, five . . .
Touché Turtle, Mr Hiccup and the Plonsters are having adventures that are really out of this world.
Four, three, two, one . . .
Tune in to *Doodle!*
Music MICHAEL OMER
Executive producer
THERESA PLUMMER-ANDREWS
Producer ROY MILANI

4.15 Jonny Briggs
Last part of a serial in 13 episodes by JOAN EADINGTON
Jonny's kite is nearly ready, when Albert's scheme for a water-balloon battle starts off with a typical disaster.
Jonny	RICHARD HOLIAN
Mam	JANE LOWE
Dad	LESLIE SCHOFIELD
Rita	SUE DEVANEY
Albert	TOMMY ROBINSON
Humphrey	JEREMY AUSTIN
Miss Broom	KAREN MEAGHER
Mr Hobbs	MICHAEL THOMAS
Mr Badger	JOHN FORBES-ROBERTSON
Pam	GEORGINA LANE
Josie	RACHEL POWELL
Jinny	ADELE PARRY
Martin	DEXTER LYNCH
and Razzle as Fizzy
Dog handler PAULINE CLIFT
Producer ANGELA BEECHING
Director CHRISTINE SECOMBE *(R)*

4.30 Pole Position
The Race (R)

5.00 Newsround

NEW SERIES
5.10 The Lowdown
First of six programmes
Real-life stories about children today, told by children themselves.
The Takeover
Imagine having the chance to run your school. For one week 13-year-old **Michael Mawdsley** did just that and took over as headmaster of Redbrook Middle School in Rochdale, helped by two friends as deputy heads.
The Lowdown shows how they survived the experience, the ups and downs of school life, and the changes they made.
Film editor CHRIS WOOLLEY
Executive producer ERIC ROWAN
Director VIVIANA WOODRUFF
● BACK PAGES: 102
★ CEEFAX SUBTITLES

5.35 Neighbours
(Shown at 1.30pm)

6.00 Six O'Clock News
with **Sue Lawley** and **Nicholas Witchell**
Weather JOHN KETTLEY

6.35 Regional news magazines
(For details see Monday)

7.00 Three Up, Two Down
by RICHARD OMMANNEY
Daphne	ANGELA THORNE
Sam	MICHAEL ELPHICK
Nick	RAY BURDIS
Angie	LYSETTE ANTHONY
Baby Joe	ALEXANDER HILL
Wilf	JOHN GRILLO
Man on the beach
CRAIG FAIRBRASS
Doctor | STEPHEN BRIGDEN
Designer RICHARD BRACKENBURY
Produced and directed by
JOHN B. HOBBS *(R)*

7.30-8.00 EastEnders
by JULIET ACE
'She's my daughter, Ian. That bitch is my flesh and blood'.
(For cast see page 71)
★ CEEFAX SUBTITLES

Head of the class: just the job for pupils Michael Mawdsley (centre), Jill Whittaker and Waheed 'Billy' Ghauri BBC1, 5.10pm The Lowdown

---

BBC 2

4.00pm
Dr Kildare
starring
Richard Chamberlain
as Dr James Kildare
Raymond Massey
as Dr Leonard Gillespie
Lee Kurty
as Nurse Zoe Lawton
with guest stars
Dean Stockwell
as Rudy Devereux
Tony Bell
as Tom Hartwood
Shetland Wells
as Frankie Warren
A Pyrotechnic Display
In this concluding episode, Kildare the teacher becomes Kildare the student, as Rudy, Tom and Frankie reach the point when they must decide between personal feelings and professional ambition. *(R) (A new story begins on Friday at 4.00pm)*

4.25
An Actor's Life for Me
A final compilation of stories about the theatre, taking in chapters on 'being off when you should be on', 'the curse of the corpse', and 'resting', which is never very restful.
With **Jenny Agutter**
Jane Asher
Richard Briers
Eleanor Bron
Judy Cornwell
Denholm Elliott
Michael Gough
Sheila Hancock
Freddie Jones
Maureen Lipman
Anna Massey
Denis Quilley
Leonard Rossiter
Jack Shepherd
Producer TONY STAVEACRE
BBC Bristol (R)

4.55 Cartoon
Mushrooms (R)

Kathy Tayler (left) tries her hand at carriage-driving helped by instructor Georgina Dale-Leech
BBC2, 5.00pm The Alternative Holiday Show

NEW SERIES
5.00 The Alternative Holiday Show
If you've always suspected that there could be more to a holiday than lying on a crowded beach, then this new series is for you.
John Thirlwell and **Kathy Tayler** look at the alternatives on offer on your doorstep and they have a go themselves.
Today, among other things, horses, history and jazz.
Director MARCEL GUILLOU
Producer MIKE MURRAY
(First shown on BBC North East)
For more information send an sae to: The Alternative Holiday Show, BBCtv, Woodhouse Lane, Leeds LS2 9PX
(Next programme tomorrow at 5.00pm)
● INFO: page 92

5.30
Gardeners' World
at Rosemoor Gardens, Torrington, North Devon
BBC Pebble Mill
(Shown last Friday)

6.00 International Pro-Celebrity Golf
Turnberry bares her teeth today as **Bruce Forsyth** and **Lee Trevino** take on the two **Sandys, Gall** and **Lyle**, for the *Whyte and Mackay Scotch Trophy*.
A howling wind gives way to sublime sunshine, and the guests Bruce and Sandy prove their mettle in the difficult conditions.
Peter Alliss also braves the elements over nine holes of the Ailsa Course at the Turnberry Hotel.
Assistant producers
DEREK MARTIN, MURRAY NEEDHAM
Television presentation
ALASTAIR SCOTT, FRED VINER
Executive producer
JOHN SHREWSBURY

New from BBC Video
The following golf videos are available from retailers
Victory in Australia: J. Walker
Ryder Cup 87, BBCV 4010
Bell's Scotch Ryder Cup 1985
BBCV 4114
PGA European Tour – 1985
Highlights, BBCV B 5030

6.50 Architecture at the Crossroads
Ten films about contemporary architecture
9: *Berlin: A City for People*
It took eight years to create Berlin's mammoth International Building Exhibition of 1987, with a cast list of contributors that reads like a *Who's Who* of contemporary architecture. Its focus was on social housing within the modern inner city. The venue for the exhibition was the city itself, real houses and building complexes, already inhabited, and designed to demonstrate how the city can once again become a place fit for people. The Berlin schemes could well become prototypes for the rest of the world, building with people rather than merely for them.
Narrator **Andrew Sachs**
Excellent with revealing perspectives
LONDON STANDARD
An impressive series
TIME OUT
Associate producer ROGER LAST
Written and produced by
PETER ADAM *(R)*
(Postponed from 10 May)

7.30-8.00 Mortimer in Tuscany
'A sunny place for shady people' – Tuscany has always been a magnet for the British escaping from their native climate and morals. **John Mortimer** is the latest in a long line of British writers from Shelley to D.H. Lawrence, to fall under the Tuscan spell. He talks to two distinguished exiles, **Sir Harold Acton** and **Muriel Spark** and to some of the lesser-known Britons who flock to Florence every year in search of enlightenment. Does Italy still have the same effect on English girls as it had on Lucy Honeychurch in E. M. Forster's *A Room with a View*?
Production assistant RACHEL FOSTER
Executive producer JOHN ARCHER
Director DAISY GOODWIN
A REVIEW special

PROGRAMMES CONTINUE OVERLEAF

4.10pm
The Telebugs
PIT OF PERIL

Bug enjoys the game, but where will it end? ‡

4.20pm
T-Bag Strikes Again
BY LEE PRESSMAN AND GRANT CATHRO

ELIZABETH ESTENSEN
JOHN HASLER
JENNIE STALLWOOD

Debbie meets up with Long John Sylvia, the pirate radio DJ, when she is mistaken for a missing pop singer, It's not long before the ship is visited by T-Bag and things begin to explode into a riot of smoke and noise. T-Shirt, who's been sent on holiday by T-Bag meets up with Debbie who is still searching for the missing number seven from the clock and with the help of Jack, Sylvia's shipmate, they contrive to get back the silver seven. ‡

T-Bag ... Elizabeth Estensen
T-Shirt ... John Hasler
Debbie ... Jennie Stallwood
Long John Sylvia ... Jan Hunt
Jack Plugg ... Ronnie Brody
DESIGNER JOHN PLANT
DIRECTOR LEON THAU
PRODUCER CHARLES WARREN
Thames Television Production

4.45pm Chatterbox [NEW]
ALED JONES
MICHAEL QUILL
JOSIE WHITE

The first-ever children's chat show. Joining Aled, Michael, Josie and a studio audience of youngsters are some very special guests. These include Jason Connery who talks about playing Robin Hood on screen and being 'James Bond's' son in real life. Aled chats to some young people who have stories of award-winning courage, while Michael and Josie launch Bar Talk with one of the country's top young skateboarders. Also on the programme are some of the young stars of Grange Hill and Brookside.

acle subtitles page 888

SEARCH MARTIN LAMB
OGRAMME ASSOCIATE
GEL CROWLE
CTOR KENNETH PRICE
ODUCERS PETER MURPHY,
NETH PRICE
Production

15pm
nner kes All
FFREY WHEELER
y McDonald

family quiz game re contestants from ver the country are ng to win the top prize.

ITN News at 5.45
FIONA ARMSTRONG
Oracle subtitles page 888

6.00pm
Thames News
Early evening round-up with John Andrew and Penny Smith.

6.25pm
Help
Community action programme with John Murray, Astrid French and Theo Sowa.

6.30 to 7.00pm
Emmerdale Farm
A moment's thoughtlessness turns a farmhouse into a death trap — and Annie Sugden walks straight into it.

This week's cast:
Annie Sugden ... Sheila Mercier
Matt Skilbeck ... Frederick Pyne
Amos Brearly ... Ronald Magill
Henry Wilks ... Arthur Pentelow
Jack Sugden ... Clive Hornby
Joe Sugden ... Frazer Hines
Dolly Skilbeck ... Jean Rogers
Sandie Merrick ... Jane Hutcheson
Jackie Merrick ... Ian Sharrock
Kathy Merrick ... Malandra Burrows
Alan Turner ... Richard Thorp
Mrs Bates ... Diana Davies
Seth Armstrong ... Stan Richards
Ruth Pennington ... Julia Chambers
Phil Pearce ... Peter Alexander
Eric Pollard ... Christopher Chittell
Archie ... Tony Pitts
Nick Bates ... Cy Chadwick
Stephen Fuller ... Gregory Floy
Jock McDonald ... Drew Dawson
Robert Sugden ... Richard Smith
WRITER JAMES ROBSON
DESIGNER JAMES O'HARE
DIRECTOR TERRY DAW
PRODUCER STUART DOUGHTY
EXECUTIVE PRODUCER KEITH RICHARDSON
Yorkshire Television Production

ITV variations
Programmes in adjoining areas are as Thames except for:

TVS 12.00 to 12.30 Bygones; 1.30 Coast to Coast People; 2.00 Country Practice; 2.30 Take the High Road; 3.00 The Krypton Factor; 3.30 to 3.57 Young Doctors; 6.00 to 6.30 Coast to Coast; 11.45 **Film — Disaster on the Coastliner.** Lloyd Bridges and Raymond Burr in gripper about two trains programmed to collide; 2.00 to 3.00am Off the Wall.

ANGLIA 12.30 to 1.00 Gardens For All; 6.00 to 6.30 About Anglia; 12.15 **Film — The Groundstar Conspiracy.** American space project is destroyed, with George Peppard; 2.00 Soap; 2.30 Hammer House of Mystery and Suspense; 4.00 to 4.35am The Jacksons.

CENTRAL 12.30 Home Cookery Club; 12.35 to 1.00 The Young Doctors; 1.30 to 2.30 Falcon Crest; 6.00 to 6.30 Central News; 12.15 **Film — Policewoman Centrefold.** Melody Anderson as a policewoman who sends photos of herself to a girlie magazine to make extra cash; 2.05 Donahue; 3.00 The Best of the Beat Club; 4.00 to 5.00am Jobfinder.

9.30am
Schools
9.30 The French Programme
France-Magazine 4: Contemporary 'politics' special.

9.52 Environments
Fair Isle — Meadow, Moor and Beach: the spectacular bird life, plants and animals on this tiny island.

10.09 All Year round
Playing With Air: (Repeat of last Thursday's programme).

10.26 Facts For Life
A studio discussion about infectious diseases.

10.48 Living and Growing
Starting A Baby: Conception, foetal development, antenatal care and contraception.

11.05 Middle English
Rose by Jan Mark: (Repeat of Tuesday's programme).

11.22 Picture Box
River of Sun and Moon: Jayne Dowell, a Liverpool teenager, describes the legends and history of the River Mersey.

11.41 Craft, Design and Technology
Fashion Sense: Jeff Banks discusses his idea for an austere 'granny' look.

12.00noon
Sesame Street
The Count discovers that he likes baseball because he can count the balls and the bats. Today's letters are U and Z and the number is 5.

12.30pm
Business Daily
SUSANNAH SIMONS

Britain's daily business and financial TV news service with computer links to City securities houses and a network of studios around the Square Mile. There is news and analysis of the main business and industrial stories of the day. With Iain Carson and reporters Jane Alexander and Tom Maddocks.

1.00pm
Jobsearch
Ten very different people: a hairdresser, a former apprentice footballer, a radiator mechanic, a housewife, a welder, a holiday courier, a receptionist, a

---

storeman, a secretary and a flour miller attend a special course to learn how to find a job. Today's programme looks at interviewing techniques. The students do a series of mock interviews and then analyse what they did wrong. A free Jobsearch pamphlet is available from C4 address 2 page 37. ‡
Oracle subtitles page 888
DIRECTOR NEIL CLEMINSON
PRODUCER BRIAN MORRIS
EXECUTIVE PRODUCER ROD CAIRD
Granada Television Production

1.30pm
Write On
RUTH PITT
IAN McMILLAN

4: NOTE AND WRITE
Writing is not a one-off exercise and this programme looks at how writers need to select their material — and perhaps have several attempts — before they are satisfied. Linked to the Open College course, 'The Writing Course', price £25 (£49.99 with tutorial support). For further information write to C4 address 2, page 37, or phone (0235) 555444. ‡
Oracle subtitles page 888
DIRECTOR IAN FELL
PRODUCER DAVID WILSON
Yorkshire Television Production

2.00pm
The Parliament Programme
Television's only programme providing up-to-the-minute coverage of the work of both Houses of Parliament on a daily basis — with live interviews, sound coverage of the proceedings of the House of Commons and television coverage of the House of Lords. Reporters are Nicholas Woolley and Jackie Ashley. Presented by Glyn Mathias.

'I Dream of Jeannie', declares Tony (Larry Hagman) — and you'll soon see why at 5.30pm

2.30pm
Eternally Yours
LORETTA YOUNG
DAVID NIVEN
BRODERICK CRAWFORD

 FILM Anita Halstead leaves her society sweetheart Don Barnes for the more exciting magician Toby. They marry and start travelling but Anita begins to yearn for a home and roots. . .

Made in black and white

See film guide, beginning page 33

Anita ... Loretta Young
Toby ... David Niven
Benton ... Hugh Herbert
Aunt Abby ... Billie Burke
Bishop Hubert Peabody ... C Aubrey Smith
Harley Bingham ... Raymond Walburn
Carrie Bingham ... ZaSu Pitts
Don ... Broderick Crawford
Lola De Vere ... Virginia Field
Gloria ... Eve Arden
Pilot ... Tay Garnett
SCREENPLAY GENE TOWNE, GRAHAM BAKER, JOHN MEEHAN
DIRECTOR TAY GARNETT

4.10pm
Sue My Lawyer
HARRY LANGDON

FILM Harry persistently pesters District Attorney O T Hill for a job. But his offer to help Hill prosecute in the Red Burton murder case lands him in ever-deepening trouble.

Made in black and white

See film guide, beginning page 33

With Harry Langdon, Anne Doran, Bud Jamison
SCREENPLAY EWART ADAMSON
FROM A STORY BY HARRY LANGDON
DIRECTOR JULES WHITE

4.30pm
Countdown
Norma Cooper, a ward sister from Stevenage, is today's challenger.

5.00pm
Ark on the Move
GERALD DURRELL

4: RESCUE FLIGHT
Birds are perhaps the most vulnerable of animals. One such bird in danger is the Mauritius pink pigeon, and Gerald Durrell penetrates an isolated forest to observe its courting and nesting behaviour. Also captured on film is the rarest bird in the world — the Mauritius kestrel. ‡
DIRECTORS ALASTAIR BROWN, MICHAEL MALTBY
PRODUCER PAULA QUIGLEY
EXECUTIVE PRODUCER PAT FERNS
Nielsen-Ferns/Primetime TV Co-production

5.30pm
I Dream of Jeannie
DJINN, DJINN, GO HOME

Jeannie's dog turns up — but he hates uniforms.

Jeannie ... Barbara Eden
Tony ... Larry Hagman
Dr Bellows ... Hayden Rorke
Roger ... Bill Daily
Gen Peterson ... Barton MacLane
Mrs Bellows ... Emmaline Henry

6.00pm
Family Ties
THE HARDER THEY FALL

Alex asks his parents to sweet talk his teacher but Elyse hits him instead.

Elyse ... Meredith Baxter Birney
Steven ... Michael Gross
Alex ... Michael J Fox
Mallory ... Justine Bateman
Jennifer ... Tina Yothers
Tedesco ... Edward Edwards

6.30 to 7.00pm
The Making of Britain
7: MASS MEDIA, MASS DEMOCRACY
Dr Paddy Scannell shows how radio and television have made democracy in Britain a reality in the 20th century. Media coverage of the great events of the day has enabled everyone in Britain to exercise their political rights in an informed way. But it has also made our cultural life much more democratic, not only bringing classical plays and music into every home but also transforming the experience of ordinary people into the subject matter for plays, soap operas and discussion in a way unimaginable 50 years ago.
PRODUCER LESLEY SMITH
DIRECTOR JOHANNA POOL
LWT Production

I'm not moving!

It's not always the children in a family who create problems. A live-in Grandma can stir up quite a few of her own, especially a Grandma who doesn't want to move. Jill Robinson's family have to shift from London to a place called Haven new town. Everyone is looking forward to the change—everyone except Gran.

Suddenly it was Friday morning. The sun was out, even if it was a bit watery. The house was upside-down, with furniture and packing cases stacked all along the hall, out through the front door and onto the pavement. There were two removal vans outside.

There seemed to be overalled men everywhere, lifting and jostling and shouting to each other. The house didn't look like our house any more.

Gran had been cheerful and seemed to be putting a brave front on things. She bustled around being helpful, and then went upstairs to pack the last of her personal belongings in a suitcase.

Then, when the furniture had gone and the very last packing cases were being taken out to the vans, something awful happened.

A fairly old removal man, struggling with an awkward box, paused for breath. He balanced it on the banister knob then said to me in a cheerful shout—

"You're the third family we've moved to Haven new town this year! Seen it? All glass and concrete it is. Frightens the life out of an old 'un like me. All right for you young people. I suppose."

Then he jerked his thumb up towards the ceiling, meaningfully.

"Surprised the old lady's going with you, though. Wouldn't have thought it's the place for old folk. A bloke I know stuck it for three weeks and then chucked it in and came back to London—"

"Do you mind—?" I began indignantly.

Then suddenly I felt an icy presence behind me.

I looked round and there was Gran, half-way down the stairs, with a little picture from our room that the men had forgotten. She'd heard every word that awful man had said!

She stood there for a few seconds, gripping the banister rail so hard that her knuckles turned white. Then, without a word, she turned and went back upstairs.

KITCHEN THINGS

FRAGILE

THIS WAY ↑ UP

The removal man whistled to himself, a bit red in the face, and carried out the box to the waiting van.

I dashed up the stairs after Gran. But even as I reached our room, I heard the key grate in the lock, inside.

"Gran! He doesn't know what he's talking about—"

"Oh, I dare say he does." From inside the room, her voice was trembling. "That's settled it. I was very foolish ever to listen to any of you. Well, I'm not coming."

"Gran! Don't be silly!" I rattled the door handle in alarm. "Unlock the door. Please let's talk! Let me in!"

"There's nothing to talk about. The door stays locked, and here in this house I stay. Just for a few days till I find some lodgings. I've no intention of shifting; not for anyone."

In no time, the whole family had joined me outside the big bedroom. We tapped and we cajoled. We knocked and we argued. But it was no use.

"This calls for a family conference," said Mum, despairingly. She led the way downstairs and we all followed her into the kitchen. There was a bag on the kitchen floor, ready to go in the car with us. 'I'll unpack the flasks and we'll have a cup of coffee."

"I just don't know how to handle this one," said Dad. "Once she gets one of these moods on she can be stubborn as a mule. She'll be up there for hours."

"Oh dear. Oh dear." Mum looked at her watch unhappily and bit her lip. "We *must* get away soon. Just imagine trying to move into Newlands Park in the dark!"

"What on earth are we going to *do*?" sighed Sarah.

There was silence.

"Let's break the door down!" exclaimed Tony suddenly.

"Don't be daft," snapped Dad, irritably.

I gazed out of the kitchen window. In the back garden two of the removal men were dismantling our ancient garden hammock on our little strip of back lawn. It was just about their last job and then they would shut up the backs of the vans and drive off.

"Got it!" I exclaimed.

"Got what, Jill?" asked Mum. They all looked at me hopefully.

"Got an idea."

I explained my idea to them. Dad thought about it.

"Hmmm."

"Corny," said Tony, rudely. "Really corny."

"Have you got a better one then?" I asked indignantly.

"I think it's a marvellous idea!" said Sarah dramatically. "It's not corny at all. It's true. The pure, unadulterated truth…"

"Course it is," I nodded.

"Hmmm," said Dad again. "Well I suppose you could say it has an element of truth in it. I—"

"Oh, come on, John," said Mum, looking at her watch again with genuine anxiety. "Why not give Jill's idea a try—?"

"Okay," said Dad.

He marched out through the back door and into the garden.

We all crowded out behind him. We were standing directly below the big bedroom at the back, Gran's and Sarah's and mine, where Gran was locked in. I glanced up and noticed that the window was open.

33

"Right, stop!" Dad bellowed loudly at the men, who had now got the hammock into several pieces on the lawn.

"Stop?" gawped the younger of the two men.

"Yes. Please put that hammock back together again."

"You leaving it here then, sir?" asked the foreman. He frowned. "I thought you said—"

"I'm leaving it here. That goes for the furniture, too. I want it all moved back into the house."

The expression on the men's faces had to be seen to be believed.

"Don't worry," Dad said. "You'll be paid for all your work."

"Are you moving or ain't you?" the foreman asked slowly.

"We're not moving," stated Dad.

"NOT MOVING?"

I glanced up at the bedroom window and thought I saw a movement.

"It's my mother, she refuses to go," said Dad. "We can't force her. It wouldn't be fair, not at her age. But we're not going to leave her in London, living on her own. So that's that. We've got to think again. About the whole thing."

"It'd be horrible to move without Gran!" I said loudly, but with real feeling, because I meant it.

"Unthinkable!" declaimed Sarah.

"We're just not going!" added Tony, cupping his hands to his mouth and glancing upwards and overdoing things a bit. *"We're staying right here... ouch!"*

I'd trodden on his toe.

The removal men clearly thought that the whole Robinson family was completely dotty. But Dad's voice was so firm and his gaze so steely that they just grumbled and mumbled and started putting the hammock together again.

We all went back into the kitchen to drink our coffee; on tenterhooks, we waited.

On the back lawn the hammock was soon reassembled and the two men were joined by the third removal man, the oldish one who had started all the trouble in the first place. They went into a huddle — glared towards the kitchen once or twice — then out round by the back lane which would take them along the backs and through to the street where their vans were parked.

Soon there was the sound of bumping in the front of the house; I peeped out and saw them bringing the sideboard back into the house. After the sideboard, with even more bumping, came two armchairs and the dining room table.

We all stood in the kitchen, looking at each other, saying nothing. The time was ticking by. I felt tense as anything. Then—

"Listen!" whispered Tony. "That was some floor-boards creaking upstairs!"

Dad tip-toed out into the hall and we all followed.

Gran appeared at the top of the stairs.

She was wearing her coat and hat and carrying her small suitcase.

Then she advanced tentatively down the stairs, her mouth quivering at the corners.

"What a lot of nonsense!" she said jerkily. "Of course we must move!" She came slowly down into our midst, all bunched at the bottom of the stairs. She fixed Dad with a funny sort of protective look. "You've worked for that firm for fifteen years. You've got a good job—and you're getting a rise as well. You're not giving all that up for me! Oh dear me, no!"

Us three and Mum just fell upon Gran and hugged and kissed her; she smiled, quiet and watery-eyed.

While the astounded removal men moved the sideboard and the dining-room table out to the vans again, Gran turned to me and gave my arm a little squeeze.

"Wait and see, Jill!" she chuckled. "I'll teach those young people in Haven a thing or two. Plenty of life in the old lady yet. Oh dear, yes!"

Written by Anne Digby
Illustrated by Cindy Hunnam

36

Mothering Sunday

The fourth Sunday in Lent is kept as Mothering Sunday. This is three weeks before Easter. In the past, people visited their nearest "Mother Church" on this day. It was traditional for the Bible story of the "Feeding of the Five Thousand" to be read at this service. Sons and daughters met up with their mothers on this Sunday.

This special day became known as "Mothering Sunday" or "Simnel Sunday". Servants and apprentices were given a day off to go home to see their mothers. They would take her a bunch of flowers or a Simnel cake. The traditional Simnel cake is spicy. It is made with fine flour, currants, peel and spices. The top is decorated with artificial flowers, nests, tiny eggs or marzipan balls.

There is a story about a servant girl whose Simnel cake was so heavy that her mother used it to kneel on in Church. She must have used the wrong flour!

Simnel cake

Mothering Sunday is often confused with Mother's Day. In 1907 an American woman, Anna Jarvis, suggested that one day in the year should be set aside for remembering and honouring all mothers. By 1913 the second Sunday in May was declared a national holiday — for "the best mother in the world — your mother." The custom was soon adopted in other countries.

During the Second World War, American soldiers brought this festival to Britain. They gave presents to their landladies on the second Sunday in May.

Today, children of all ages send cards and give presents to their mother on Mother's Day. In Britain this is on Mothering Sunday — the fourth Sunday in Lent. In America, Canada and Australia, Mother's Day is on the second Sunday in May.

John Dark and Other Homework

Thirteen-year-old Karen Sossi hasn't been doing too well lately, particularly at school. Life isn't made easier by the fact that her older sister, Elaine, always gets top marks in everything. Even nine-year-old Aldo seems to be able to cope better than she can and he has his best friend, De De, to talk things over with. Karen hasn't anyone to confide in. It's hard not to feel sorry for herself.

Homework was a pain, Karen thought. No matter what she was doing these days, in the back of her mind there was always the nagging reminder of undone homework. She had to write a weekly composition for English, and she had to come up with an idea for a science project that would be due in December. Both subjects bored her to tears. She wished she didn't have to go to school and could just stay home and do the things she wanted.

The funny thing, though, was that what she most enjoyed doing was *real* homework. She loved experimenting in the kitchen with a new recipe. Elaine, who was very good at school subjects, hated to spend any time in the kitchen unless she was eating there.

So, although she should have been doing homework for school, Karen spent several hours each weekend in the kitchen, cooking or baking something new. Today she was making two loaves of whole-wheat bread. She had never baked bread before, but it turned out to be quite simple and a lot of fun. Working with yeast was not nearly as difficult as she had anticipated. Making the dough and punching it into shape was fun.

Elaine stuck her head into the kitchen and asked, "Who are you pretending that you're hitting?"

"My maths teacher. She's a witch," said Karen, but at that moment she really didn't mean it. She was enjoying herself too much to worry about her maths teacher or her science teacher or her English teacher.

"Just be sure that you clean up any mess that you make," Mrs Sossi said. She always said the same thing. Karen was pretty good about cleaning up, and sometimes if Aldo and his friend De De were around, she could bribe them with some of her finished goods to help her with the clean-up.

Finally the bread dough was set in a bowl to rise. Walking out of the kitchen, Karen saw her father was watching a football game in the living room. Mrs Sossi was nowhere to be seen. Karen suspected that she had gone to another garage sale in town. Her mother spent many Sunday afternoons that way; she was always hunting for bargains.

Karen went upstairs and saw Aldo through the open door of his room. He was moping on his bed. "What's up?" she asked him.

"I just remembered that I have to give a report on John Dark tomorrow, and I forgot to go to the library."

"You should plan ahead," said Karen, quoting her mother. How many times a week did she hear those words? "Anyhow, who is John Dark?"

"He's a famous person. Everyone in my class picked a different person to do a report on," said Aldo.

"I never heard of him," said Karen, shrugging her shoulders. "He can't be that famous."

"I know. He isn't even in the encyclopaedia. I looked," Aldo sighed.

"It's not the most up-to-date set," Karen agreed, referring to the encyclopaedia published in 1962 that her mother had recently bought at a garage sale.

"Maybe you didn't do it right," she suggested hopefully. "I'll help you."

The two of them went to the hallway bookshelf that held the set of books. They had only cost ten dollars, so they were a real bargain, except that everything Karen or Elaine or Aldo wanted to look up seemed to have happened after 1962. Probably John Dark had become famous since then too. Karen wondered if he was an astronaut.

She turned to the *D* volume, but there was nothing there. "See," said Aldo. "I told you there wasn't anything."

"What do you know about John Dark?" asked Karen.

"Nothing."

"Don't you have any idea why he is famous? Was he a scientist?"

"I don't know," said Aldo.

"Did he invent something?"

"I don't know."

"Do you think he was in politics?" asked Karen.

"I don't know," said Aldo helplessly. "The teacher called out a bunch of names, and each of us chose one to do a report on. When she said John Dark, I raised my hand. I guess I should have picked Louis the Fourteenth."

"Louis the Fourteenth?" said Karen. "What other names were there?"

"Marie Antoinette. That's who De De picked. And other famous people from French history."

"French history," said Karen. "I bet Elaine would know!"

Elaine was just getting ready to leave the house. "Did you ever hear of a man named John Dark?" asked Karen.

"Nope," said Elaine, zipping her jacket.

"Aldo says John Dark was important in French history," said Karen. "I thought you knew everything about France and things French."

Elaine thought a moment. "John Dark?" she said. "Jeanne d'Arc! Of course I've heard of *her*. That's the French way of saying Joan of Arc. Boy, you really are stupid if you thought she was a man!" she said, as she slammed the door behind her.

Karen was so pleased that the mystery of John Dark was solved that she wasn't offended by Elaine's words. She rushed back to Aldo, who was thumbing his way through the pages of the *D* volume of the encyclopaedia. "It's Jeanne d'Arc," she said. "You volunteered to write about Jeanne d'Arc."

"That's what I said," said Aldo. "John Dark."

Karen reached for the *A* volume. Since she didn't have a last name, the French heroine was probably listed under Arc. she turned the pages without success.

"This encyclopaedia is no good," complained Aldo.

"Wait," said Karen. "Let me look under *J*."

"I learned that people are always under their last names in the encyclopaedia," said Aldo.

"I know," said Karen. "I learned that too. But sometimes teachers are wrong," she said hopefully. Sure enough, there in the *J* volume was a long article about Joan of Arc. "Look," she said triumphantly pointing to a picture. "That's Jeanne d'Arc."

"You mean John Dark is a woman!" Aldo gasped, gaping at the drawing in the book in front of him. "That's how he spells his name?" he asked.

"Sure," said Karen. "In French, Jeanne d'Arc is pronounced like John Dark. And she was very famous. Even I've heard of her."

"Now I really am in trouble," said Aldo.

"What's the problem?" asked Karen. "Boys can write reports on women. It's no big deal."

"That's what you think," said Aldo. "We're supposed to dress up like our historical figure and tell about his life. How can I dress up like a lady?"

Karen started laughing. "What did your teacher say when you picked Jeanne d'Arc?" she asked.

"She just said, 'That will be interesting to see.' But I didn't know what she meant."

"Ohhhhhh, wait! I forgot my bread," said Karen, and she rushed off to the kitchen. Anxiously she checked the large bowl filled with dough. Sure enough, just as the instructions said, the dough had increased in quantity during the time she had been spending with Aldo. She punched it some more and once again covered it with a damp towel.

"It sure doesn't look like bread," said Aldo. "Maybe you did something wrong."

"Be patient," said Karen.

They left the kitchen and began discussing Jeanne d'Arc. Aldo phoned his friend De De for suggestions. "Stop laughing," he scolded her over the phone.

"She's going to make a fake head and pretend that she got her head cut off, because that really happened to Marie Antoinette," he told Karen, after he hung up. "I wish I could do something neat like that."

"There must be something you can do too," Karen consoled Aldo. "Just don't set your classroom on fire!" She thought some more and turned to look at the pages about Jeanne d'Arc in the encyclopaedia again.

"Let me go and put the bread into the oven, and then I'll tell you what to do," said Karen. "I think I have an idea."

Karen returned from the kitchen carrying a roll of aluminium foil. "Here," she said. "We can use this. Bring me a wire clothes hanger, an old sheet, a candlestick with a candle, and a baseball bat."

"You sound like Cinderella's fairy godmother," said Aldo, puzzled over this peculiar list of objects. "Next you'll want me to bring you two white rats. I think you'd better stick to making bread."

"No, no," said Karen. "It will work. You'll see."

Aldo ran about the house getting the needed supplies.

"I thought of something else," said Karen, when he had assembled all the things on the floor of his room. "Get your woollen ski hat. The one that Grandma knitted you last winter and you never want to wear."

Aldo dug into his bottom drawer and found the hat. "It itches," he complained. "I don't like it."

47

"That's OK. It's perfect for the purpose," said Karen. "Look." She pointed to the picture of Jeanne d'Arc in the encyclopaedia. "That ski hat is just like the helmet that she wore. Now when it's time for your report, turn off the lights in the classroom and light a candle for atmosphere. Then put the sheet around you and the ski cap on your head, and you can say that you are the ghost of Jeanne d'Arc."

"What about the baseball bat?" asked Aldo.

"Cover that with aluminium foil, and it will be your sword."

"Hey, that's great," said Aldo. "In the dark, I won't mind being a woman so much either."

"Besides, if you read about her, you'll see that she was very brave and special. And you know, she even became a saint."

"What's the hanger for?" asked Aldo. "To hang up the sheet after I use it?"

"No, no," said Karen. "Here," she said, picking it up. "If you pull it out of shape and wrap it with foil, you can make it into a halo. Then, just before you finish your talk, you can hold it over your head by the hook and explain that you have been made into a saint."

"That's fantastic," said Aldo. "Thanks for helping me. I know I'll get a good mark now."

Karen glanced at her wristwatch. "Let's go check the bread. It should be ready by this time."

The odour of the baking bread filled the house. The smell was wonderful. Considering that the house had been so quiet before, the kitchen was suddenly filled. Elaine, who had been in such a hurry to rush off before, had reappeared on the scene.

It was half time at the football game, and Mr Sossi came into the kitchen looking for a snack. Mrs Sossi was sitting in the kitchen going through the contents of a paper shopping bag and eager to show off her purchases. "Look," she said proudly, holding up a small dish. "This is a Wedgwood ashtray, and it cost only twenty-five cents." Since none of them smoked, none of them was properly interested.

No one looked at Mrs Sossi. Everyone was looking at Karen's bread. Even the family cats, Peabody and Poughkeepsie, had come into the kitchen, and they didn't even eat bread. The two brown loaves looked wonderful, but they smelt even better.

"We have to let them cool," said Karen.

'I can't wait," said Elaine, taking the butter out of the refrigerator. Aldo reached for the jar of peanut butter in the cupboard, and Mr Sossi took out a jar of apricot jam. Mrs Sossi got some cream cheese. When they all had their own favourite spread ready, they refused to wait any longer.

Karen took a knife and began slicing into one of the loaves. She knew she should wait a little longer until it had cooled, but she was just as eager as the rest of her family to see how the bread had turned out.

"It sure looks like real bread," said Aldo.

"But how does it taste?" asked Karen.

The replies weren't very clear, because everyone had a mouthful of food. But heads went up and down in agreement. Hands went out for seconds.

"Karen," said Aldo, when his mouth was empty enough to speak, "you're a genius! First John Dark and now this. You're great!"

Karen thought of the report card she would be getting one of these days. It wouldn't be the card of a genius.

"John Dark? Who is John Dark?" asked Mrs Sossi.

"He's an important woman that I have to do a report on, and Karen helped me. I bet I get an A because of Karen," said Aldo happily. He reached for another slice of bread.

"Karen has the perfect fifth-grade mind," said Elaine. "Too bad she's in eighth grade."

Karen stuck her tongue out at Elaine and pulled the second loaf of bread away from her before she could cut into it. She wrapped it in the piece of aluminium foil that Aldo had left after making his sword and halo. The bread would make good sandwiches for lunch to-morrow.

Written by Johanna Hurwitz
Illustrated by Maria Yeap

Fascinating Facts About Bread

People discovered how to make bread thousands of years ago. At first, they made flat cakes which they baked on heated rocks. Then, probably by accident, they found that if the dough was left in a warm, dark place something strange happened. It began to grow higher and higher. The dough had fermented causing gas bubbles which had pushed up the dough into a round shape. When they baked this puffed-up dough it was soft and full of tiny holes. Much nicer than all those flat, hard cakes they'd been eating!

Nowadays, we use yeast to make the bread rise. It encourages the bacteria to get to work and make the dough ferment. This is called leavening. Kneading or punching the dough makes it rise higher and makes for lighter, softer bread.
Unleavened bread, like damper, is made from flour and water or milk and is cooked straight away. Australia's early settlers and explorers didn't have time to wait for the dough to rise, so they made their bread in the old way and cooked it in the hot ashes of campfires.

The word lady comes from the Anglo-Saxon word llaef-dige meaning 'loaf-maker'.

No one knows for sure where the word damper came from. Most believe it was an old English word for snack — something to 'dampen' the hunger pains.

Johnny cakes (something you hear about in folk tales and songs) were really journey cakes. Flat damper-like cakes, large enough to do for each day of the journey.

In Jewish homes, unleavened bread is always served at the Feast of the Passover. This is in memory of the flight of the Jews from Egypt in Old Testament times, when the fleeing families had no time to wait for their bread to rise.

Do you know what side your bread is buttered on?

51

BROWN BLISS-BLESSED BREAD

Ingredients: *(Say that quickly ten times over!)*

1 cup lukewarm water
1 tablespoon dry yeast
¼ cup maple syrup or honey
½ cup oil

4½ cups wholemeal flour
1 level teaspoon seasalt
2 teaspoons dried rosemary
1 egg beaten wildly

HELP!

Method

Place lukewarm water in large bowl and sprinkle in yeast.
Stir lightly until yeast has dissolved.

Add maple syrup and oil. Cover bowl and leave to rest until yeast starts
bubbling. (*Not long! — about 20 minutes*)

In a separate bowl, mix dry ingredients together (seasalt, rosemary and
wholemeal flour).

Stir dry ingredients into yeast and warm-water mixture.
Now tip onto a lightly-floured board.

Knead for 10 minutes with two clean hands. (*Ask your teacher how to
pummel the dough!*)

Lightly oil large bowl (*so dough won't stick*), and put dough back in it.
Cover bowl with clean tea towel and put in a warm spot to rise. Give it a
couple of hours. It should double in size if it's warm enough.

I'M RISING TO
THE OCCASION

Meanwhile, oil a baking tin. When dough has risen, put it in loaf tin and
punch it down a bit.

With a sharp knife, make a few slits in the top of the dough. You can
either give it a chance to rise again naturally or if you're impatient like me,
brush the top with beaten egg and bake for one hour at 180°C.

HELP! I NEED
A HAND TO GET
OUT OF HERE!

YUM! YUM! REAL
FRESH BROWN
BREAD COMING UP!

52

HOW MUCH?
MEASURING VOLUME

It's impossible to cook without measuring. And liquids are measured differently from solids. Instead of grams we use millilitres. If the recipe needs only a small amount of liquid you may be told to use half a teaspoon, or perhaps three tablespoons. If there is a lot, the measurement will be given in litres. Medicine measures, however, are usually marked in millilitres.

The word *litre* comes from a Greek word meaning a measure of weight. *Milli* comes from the Latin word *mille* which means a thousand. (The word *mile* also came from the Latin language and used to mean one thousand paces.)

Old recipes give measurements that were dropped when the metric system was adopted. Some of them have interesting meanings.

Pint A word that probably comes from a Spanish word *pincta* which meant a container that was painted or marked. The mark showed what level you needed to measure exactly one pint.

Quart A quart was two pints or a quarter of a gallon. And quarter came from the Latin word *quartus*, meaning one-fourth.

Gallon This word comes from an old French word *galon* which meant the kind of bowl used to hold the goods to be measured.

UGH!

—30ML—
—15ML—
—10ML—
—5ML—
—2·5ML—

I'M MILLY PEDE

Were you a witch, Jeanne d'Arc?

Who was Jeanne d'Arc?

Jeanne d'Arc, or Joan of Arc as the English called her, was the daughter of Jacques and Isabelle d'Arc who lived in the village of Domremy in northern France. Joan was born on 6th January 1412, a time when the French king, Charles VI, and the English king, Henry V, were fighting over who was to rule France.

What did she do?

She went to war, that's what! Even more, in an age when women never wore men's clothing or had anything to do with fighting, Joan donned a suit of armour and led the soldiers into battle — and they won!

Mind you, she was an unusual girl. From the time she was thirteen, she said she had heard voices and seen visions of angels and saints who all begged her to help France throw out the English. She was seventeen when the city of Orléans was besieged by the enemy. Joan decided it was time to act. Dressed in a page's clothes, she made her way to the headquarters of Charles VII, son of the now dead French king. Charles had never been crowned for although Henry V was dead too, the English still said France belonged to them.

Joan pleaded with Charles to let her help, saying that she had been sent to him by God. Although suspicious of her at first, Charles finally agreed, and so the young country girl became a soldier. The English believed she was in league with the devil, but the French soldiers believed, just as strongly, that they were under heavenly protection. The siege was ended, the English defeated, and two months later Charles was finally crowned King of France. Joan stood proudly by his side. But Charles lost interest in the brave youngster. He was also jealous of her popularity with the people. In the following year, when Joan was captured by French who were loyal to the English, Charles did nothing to help her.

She was sold to the English for ten thousand pounds and, in a court run by French churchmen, was tried as a witch and found guilty. At first, she was sentenced to life imprisonment. But Joan stubbornly kept saying that the voices she heard came from God, so the Church handed her over to the government for execution. She was burned alive in the public square of Rouen on 31st May 1431. She was only nineteen years old.

Joan was often described as the *Maid of Orléans*. She was made a saint in 1920.

55

Fanny's sister

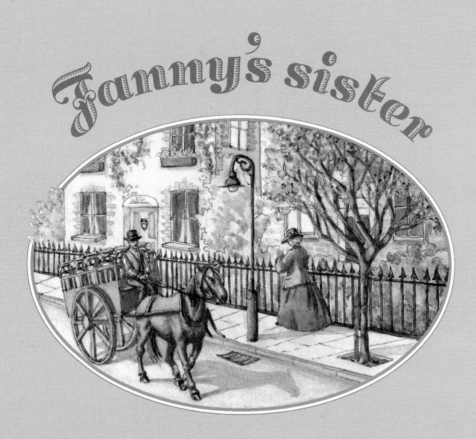

FANNY DREAMED that a cat was mewing outside her door. Be quiet, she said to it crossly, in her sleep, be quiet or you'll wake me up. The dream dissolved and she woke, warmly buried in her own bed, with a bright crack of light down the middle of the curtains telling her that it was morning. Outside, the milkman's pony clopped along the road, and a voice (Cook's, it must be, or Nellie the kitchen-maid perhaps) called out to him from the back door.

And something was mewing. But not a cat. Fanny sat bolt upright in bed, and listened. She knew that noise. It was the noise that started up afresh, next door in the nursery, as regularly, it seemed to Fanny, as Christmas and Easter and birthdays. Last year when she was eight and the year before when she was seven and the year before ... well, nearly every year anyway, because Fanny was the eldest and then there were Albert and Emma and Harriet and Charles and Jane and Susan.

56

It was the noise of a new baby. A brand new, just-born baby. In there, thought Fanny, sitting up in bed freezing in her flannel nightie, and glaring at the closed door between the night-nursery and the day-nursery, in there, tucked up in the cradle, was a new baby, red of face and loud of voice. Mamma, who had been not-very-well for weeks and weeks so that you must not jump and shout on the stairs, would be lying pale and smiling in the big bed and presently Fanny and Albert and all the others would be taken in one by one to say good morning in hushed voices and give her one quiet and gentle kiss before they went away again. And in the nursery there would be that mewing noise, night and day, with Nurse all cross and busy at the washing steaming in front of the fire, and no time for stories after tea. Her huge, white-aproned lap would be occupied by the new baby, as it had been occupied by last-year's baby (Susan) and the baby of the year before that and the year before that. Once upon a time, a long time ago, in a time that seemed all golden and glorious, like pictures of Heaven in Fanny's Bible, that lap had been Fanny's place. There she had sat, and listened to stories and had squares of hot buttered toast popped into her mouth. And then there had come Albert and the lap had been only partly hers, and then Emma and it was no longer hers at all and presently she found herself pushed upwards into the schoolroom, to Miss Purser with her rabbity teeth and her ruler that tapped your knuckles if you did not pay attention, and her horrible, horrible sums.

I hate babies, said Fanny to the picture of an angel on the wall at the foot of her bed, and the angel, its halo exploding into a fiery sky, stared disapprovingly back, because nice little girls do not hate anything, least of all their dear little brothers and sisters.

The door opened. The hump of bedclothes in the next bed that was Emma sat up and said she was hungry for breakfast.

"All in good time," said Nurse. She drew the curtains and light came into the room, and a blackbird's song, and the church bells ringing. It must be Sunday, thought Fanny, and alongside the crossness that the mewing noise had brought came a further crossness at the thought of Sunday. Sunday meant church, and learning by heart a passage from the Bible, and no noisy games, and more church, and repeating the passage from the Bible to Papa in his study. I hate Sundays, said Fanny to the angel, and the angel raised its eyes to the fiery sky in horror and disbelief.

Now everybody was awake. Susan began to cry and Nurse picked her up and started to dress her. "Come along now, Fanny," she said, "up you get. Don't you want to see what a nice surprise there is for you in the nursery?"

No, said Fanny silently.

"I know," said Albert, "there is a new baby. The new baby has come. Is it a boy or a girl?"

"A lovely little girl," said Nurse. She put Susan on the floor to crawl around and set about brushing Harriet's hair, briskly, taking no notice of Harriet's loud protesting noises. "A little sister for you."

"Hurray!" said Emma, and Albert groaned theatrically until Nurse snapped at him to be quiet.

"Did God send the new baby?" said Harriet, wriggling under the hairbrush, and Nurse said yes, God sent the new baby and in church today they must all say thank you to Him. "What's the matter with you, Fanny?" she went on, whipping clothes out of drawers. "Get up and put on your Sunday dress."

"I feel ill," said Fanny. "I have . . . I have a stomach-ache. And my throat is sore. And my legs hurt," she added. If you were going to do a thing you might as well do it properly. Nurse herself said that, almost every day.

"Let me see your tongue," said Nurse. And then, "Get up this minute. I never heard such nonsense."

Fanny got up, scowling, and scowled her way into her tight, stiff Sunday dress and boots and then into the nursery where Sukie the nursery-maid was ladling porridge into bowls. In the cradle by the fire the new baby mewed and Nurse picked it up and talked to it and then took it away upstairs to Mamma. Fanny burned her tongue on her porridge and kicked Albert under the table, half by accident and half on purpose, so that Albert kicked back and there was a fight, and when Nurse returned Albert was sent to stand in one corner of the room and Fanny in the other.

"Birds in their little nests agree," said Nurse. "You can stop there now, the pair of you, till I say." And Fanny, staring sullenly at the wallpaper, thought that Nurse couldn't know all that much about birds. What about baby cuckoos, she thought? They push all the other little birds out so that there's only them left. Clever cuckoos, she said to herself, and behind her, at the table, last year's baby (Susan) spattered her breakfast on the floor and howled.

Breakfast ended. Fanny and Albert were released from their corners. Nurse scolded them again and said that badly-behaved children would not be allowed to go upstairs before church and see their Mamma. Then the Old Children (Fanny, Albert and Emma) were sent to the schoolroom to write out the Sunday text and learn it by heart to recite to Papa while the Young Children (all the rest) were taken off by Sukie to be cleaned and put into outdoor clothes and packed into the donkey-cart for an airing. Fanny wished, and not for the first time, that she was still one of the Young Children.

In the schoolroom, a bluebottle, trapped like Fanny, buzzed fretfully against the window. Fanny opened her exercise book and wrote the date at the top of a clean page: Sunday 6 September 1865. In the middle of the green baize tablecloth was a sheet of paper on which Papa had written in his neat sloping handwriting the verses from the Bible that they were to copy out and learn.

She looked out of the window down into the street outside
the house, where she could see Hobbs the groom standing
beside the donkey-cart, holding the donkey while the Young
Children were loaded into the cart, two at each side. They
all looked happy and excited and Fanny, watching them,
remembered what it used to feel like jogging down the lanes,
holding on to the wooden sides of the donkey-cart with both
hands, while Nurse led the donkey and the donkey's furry
ears twitched against the flies. It's not fair, thought Fanny in
a rage, it just isn't fair.

At last Nurse came to fetch them to get ready for church. When they were washed and brushed they went down into the hall to wait for Papa to come from his study and take them to see Mamma. Fanny, her hands clasped inside her fur muff (she liked her Sunday muff, it was the only thing that was agreeable about Sundays) heard the door open on the floor above and his footsteps coming down the stairs, and then there was his large, black figure above her, complete with shiny black Sunday hat, and the gold watch-chain stretched across his waistcoat. When she was very young she had longed to pull that watch-chain but had never dared because Papa was not the kind of person to whom you could ever, ever do such a thing. Fanny loved her father, and she thought him extremely grand and important, but he seemed somehow very far away, even though she lived in the same house with him and always had done. Loving him was more like loving God or the Queen than loving, for instance, Nurse, or Jupiter the sheepdog or the donkey or even Mamma, who was also grand and a little far away but not nearly so far away as Papa.

Mamma, this morning, lay in bed in the big upstairs bedroom like a piece of precious china cocooned in tissue paper. She smiled and kissed each of them and asked what they thought of their new little sister. Emma said that she was nice and Albert said that she was nice but it was a pity she had not been a boy.

"Come now, Fanny," said Papa, "have you lost your tongue? What do you think?"

"She makes a lot of noise," said Fanny in a sullen voice, and Mamma and Papa both laughed and said that all babies cry and that was perfectly natural. Outside, the church bells were ringing, which made Papa take his watch from his waistcoat pocket and say that it was time to go.

Walking to church, Fanny forgot her irritation about the new baby. There was a dog-fight at the end of their street, which was exciting and interesting, and blackberries to pick in the hedge along the lane (quickly, behind Papa's back, cramming them into her mouth before he could see) and her best enemy, Clara Binns the doctor's daughter, outside the

church gates. Fanny and Clara stuck out their tongues at each other, as far as they would go, while Papa removed his hat to Mrs Binns and Mrs Binns inquired after Mamma and sent effusive messages of congratulations and affection.

"Shall I say thank you to God for the new baby, Papa?" said Emma, and Papa smiled and patted Emma's head and said yes, that would be very nice. And all Fanny's crossness came flowing back.

Written by Penelope Lively
Illustrated by Jane Johnson

Pages from Semolina Smith's Diary

Good things about families

1. There are others to take turns with when doing the dishes.

2. You've always got someone to blame for not feeding the cat.

3. You get plenty of birthday and Christmas presents- if you're a big family like us.

4. There's always someone with you in the bedroom when there's thunder and lightning. Even if they're as scared as you, it's good to have company.

5. You feel proud when your brothers always win the prizes for being the best footballers.

6. There's nearly always someone to do things with in the holidays.

7. When other kids pick on you, your brothers and sisters stick up for you. (Even the little ones do it.)

8. Your home is comfortable because your parents have given up telling everyone not to put their feet on the furniture.

Bad things about families

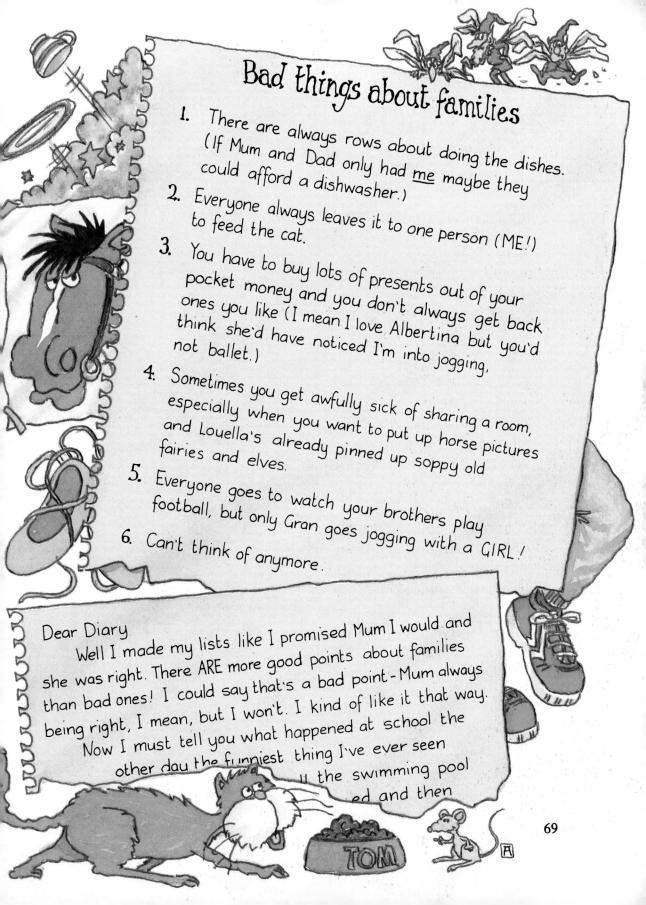

1. There are always rows about doing the dishes. (If Mum and Dad only had <u>me</u> maybe they could afford a dishwasher.)

2. Everyone always leaves it to one person (ME!) to feed the cat.

3. You have to buy lots of presents out of your pocket money and you don't always get back ones you like (I mean I love Albertina but you'd think she'd have noticed I'm into jogging, not ballet.)

4. Sometimes you get awfully sick of sharing a room, especially when you want to put up horse pictures and Louella's already pinned up soppy old fairies and elves.

5. Everyone goes to watch your brothers play football, but only Gran goes jogging with a GIRL!

6. Can't think of anymore.

Dear Diary

Well I made my lists like I promised Mum I would and she was right. There ARE more good points about families than bad ones! I could say that's a bad point - Mum always being right, I mean, but I won't. I kind of like it that way. Now I must tell you what happened at school the other day the funniest thing I've ever seen ... the swimming pool ... ed and then

Somewhere.

It's somewhere round the corner
Or so I've heard them say
And everybody wants to go
But no one knows the way.

The days are full of summer
And staying by the sea.
There's apple pie for breakfast
And what you like for tea.

And even running messages
Can be a lot of fun
While washing's not compulsory
And hair can stay undone.

Where chocolates are handy;
Please take another box.
Where only older people
Have mumps or chickenpox.

Where teachers are well hidden
And if you want the truth,
The dentist is forbidden
To touch another tooth.

The people spend their evenings
By walking on their hands
While motorcars are driven
By mostly rubber bands.

And there will be no shrieking
On what a child should do
With parents never speaking
Unless they're spoken to.

With never smell of cartridge
For guns are out of bounds.
Oh happy is the partridge
While foxes chase the hounds.

Where every tree is singing;
Where every bird is free.
With apple pie for breakfast
And what you like for tea.

No television cricket;
No giving up my chair.
I'd like to buy a ticket
If only I knew where.

Max Fatchen

71

Meet a Poet

Name: Max Fatchen

Born at: Angle Vale, South Australia

on: 3rd August, 1920

Started school at: Angle Vale,

Favourite subjects: Composition, reading, geography.

Liked best: Poetry

Hated most: Sums, handicrafts

Favourite food when young: Sticky buns, sausage rolls

Favourite food now: Cream buns, green jelly

Best-loved story or book when young: The Wind in the Willows.

Max Fatchen

Favourite types of books now: Collected poems of John Batjeman (Adult) Sun on the Stubble (Colin Thiele) Children

Three things I love: The sound of rain, steam trains, quiet rivers (Oh! And my poodle!)

Three things I hate: Bossy people, dial switches on our telly, unexpected visitors

Secret wish: To live on a riverboat

Favourite riddle or joke: Why did the beetroot blush? Because it saw the salad dressing

Ethnic background — parents: Australia

— grandparents: Australia.

Autograph: Max Fatchen

The ANT and the GRASSHOPPER

A fable by **AESOP**, adapted by **PAT EDWARDS**, Illustrated by **PETER FOSTER**.

Once there was a grasshopper who loved to sing and dance.

When he was tired, he slept in the sun.

75

Now the grasshopper spent every day frantically searching for food.

He grew thin and weak. He couldn't have danced even if he had wanted to.

Shivering and coughing, he made his way to the anthill.

But the ants were not sympathetic.

And they slammed the door on him.

So the grasshopper died in the cold winter months, while the ant family lived well on the food they had collected all summer.

Rules for Healthy Eating

1 Go for variety in your meals.

2 Avoid salty, sugary and fatty foods.

3 Watch out for chemical junk hidden in manufactured food, preservatives, colourings, etc.

4 Eat sensibly, e.g. warming foods in winter and cooling foods in summer.

5 Avoid eating large meals late at night.

6 Chew your food well and relax.

7 Don't overeat.

8 Enjoy your food.

9 Be thankful that you have enough food. Millions don't!

10 Remember, all food is OK if eaten in moderation.

Proverbs
Rules for Living

If an apple a day keeps the doctor away - what will some garlic do?

Keep EVERYONE away of course!

Proverbs are usually described as wise sayings. Most of them are very old and have been handed down as warnings or as rules for living. Here's a sample:

An apple a day keeps the doctor away.

Always save for a rainy day.

A little help is worth a lot of pity.

A stitch in time saves nine.

You can't have your cake and eat it.

We never miss the water till the well runs dry.

Early to bed, early to rise,
Makes you healthy, wealthy and wise.

Prevention is better than cure.

First come first served.

Bread is the staff of life.

My Mum always said... 'Curiosity killed the Cat'

81

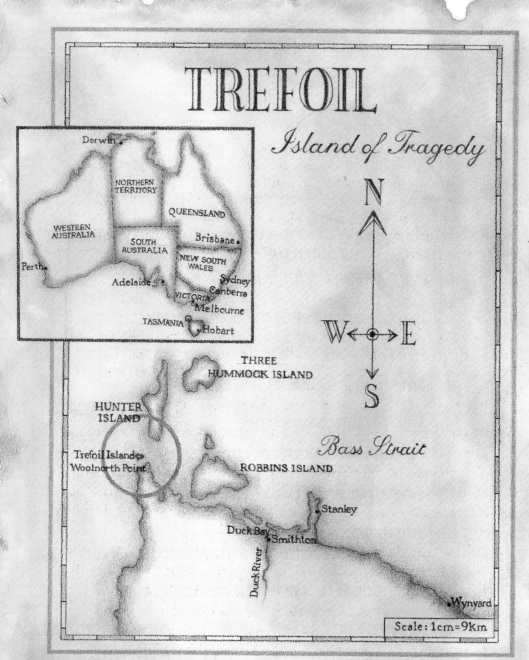

TREFOIL

Island of Tragedy

Darwin

NORTHERN
TERRITORY

QUEENSLAND

WESTERN
AUSTRALIA

SOUTH
AUSTRALIA

Brisbane

Perth

NEW SOUTH
WALES

Adelaide

Sydney
Canberra

VICTORIA
Melbourne

TASMANIA
Hobart

N
W E
S

THREE
HUMMOCK ISLAND

HUNTER
ISLAND

Bass Strait

Trefoil Island
Woolnorth Point

ROBBINS ISLAND

Stanley

Duck Bay
Smithton

Duck River

Wynyard

Scale: 1cm = 9Km

The word 'trefoil' means a three-leafed plant. It comes from the Latin words
'tres' meaning 'three' and 'folium' meaning 'leaf'.
   Matthew Flinders named Trefoil Island because its shape was like a clover
leaf. This was in 1798, when he and George Bass circumnavigated Tasmania in
a small ship called the Norfolk.

TREFOIL
Island of Tragedy

The year is 1895. The date, 14 October. Six children have been left alone on remote Trefoil Island in Bass Strait. Their normal home was a farm on Duck River on the Tasmanian mainland, but because their father, Albert Kay, leased Trefoil to run sheep on, they had moved to the island for lambing time.

Tragedy had struck when their parents, together with 16-year-old Walter and 3-year-old Sarah, were drowned while rowing from the island back to Woolnorth Point. The children had watched, horrified, unable to do anything. Now Belinda who is 13, finds herself in charge of Lydia, 12, Albert, 9, Jane, 7, Wintena, 5 and Robert, 2. Her mother, Maria, had especially asked her to care for Robert.

There's little hope of rescue before Mr Parker arrives with the shearers at the end of the year. However, desperately hoping that her father at least might have made it to nearby Bird Island, Belinda decided that they must keep fires burning on the highest point of the island.

It was a forlorn hope, for lonely Trefoil lies far from any shipping lanes . . .

After the tragedy, the children didn't clamber any more for fun and joy over the rocks. They didn't search again for nautilus shells, or the shiny pebbles of the shingle. They didn't notice at early dawn, one or other of each pair of muttonbirds fly off to fish for krill for the sitting mate; or the birds return, if they'd managed a catch, in the last light of evening.

The fires kept the children occupied, but after a time, they stoked only one blaze. It required too much physical effort to keep two fires burning all day and as far into the night as the little ones would agree to stay in the darkness, the sea drift, and the cold wind. Besides, Belinda felt they should use what large pieces of wood they found for a very different purpose. For the making of coffins.

If the bodies of their loved ones were washed ashore, they had to be prepared to receive them. She couldn't entertain the thought of those bodies not being decently buried. She expected to find even her father's body. She didn't believe he could reach Bird Island and she expected that the turn and twist of the tide would cast him up on Trefoil.

Belinda and Albert and Lydia somehow made the rough boxes that were to hold these loved ones. They made them out of driftwood and the pieces of the packing-cases in which their provisions had been brought to the island. And then, instead of clambering over the rocks for the fun of it, and searching for sea treasure, they climbed each day in search of the bodies of mother, father, sister and brother. They carried with them blankets for shrouds.

One morning they found pieces of wood from the skiff. They knew it was their boat by the colour of the paint and the fact that these pieces of wood looked newer than those that had been long in the water. The younger ones began to cry again, for they realized that what the sea had done to the boat, it had done also to their missing family. But they searched harder, if it were possible, for the bodies.

The seventh day was a particularly sad day. It would have been Sarah's fourth birthday. They mourned afresh for Sarah.

But they found no bodies.

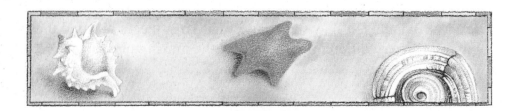

Sometimes the younger children, for whom death was yet both real and unreal, discovered something to laugh about as they traversed the island. There were many new lambs, babies—their woolly tails almost reached the ground and verily concertinaed with joy at just being alive. They took jumps into the air, and fun bursts of speed through the poa tufts, playing and gambolling in ecstasy of contentment in this place where there was nought to harm them. Or they butted their mother cheekily for a warm drink of milk, and when a mother had twins it was doubly humorous.

Robert loved the lambs. He was ready to play and laugh and gambol with them, for the day of the drowning was receding from him. It was only at night that he cried for his mother and then Belinda cuddled him hard but didn't cry with him. She knew she couldn't afford to cry with him.

"Never a ship," Albert sighed one day. "Do you think anyone will ever come, Belinda?"

"Mr Parker will come at the end of the year," she said.

"Muttonbirders?"

"Not for some time yet. Not until after Christmas."

The days when storm boomed and tore at the island were hard days to bear. It wasn't possible then to go searching among the rocks for the bodies, or collect fuel for the signal fires. The sheep and the lambs clustered miserably together for comfort, and the fires went out. The children then were confined to the hut and Belinda could only keep them occupied and not grouching by having them help her make the bread, or sew some of the garments that her mother had already cut out from the bolts of material she had brought with her. Maria had planned that the long days on the island would not be wasted and that, with so many daughters to be taught to sew, they would go home with a quantity of hand-stitched garments.

Belinda now saw to it, too, that the little hut was kept in some sort of order. Their mother had always kept their home orderly and was strict about the way certain chores must be done. Belinda felt that to show their love, they must do the same.

Most days Belinda made bread. She had seen her mother do it over and over again and she had often helped. But now she had to do it all herself, or at least most of it, while letting the little ones knead the dough if they wanted. They liked the part of folding over one end, pressing it hard down, turning the blob of dough around and around, repeating the exercise in a wheel-like movement. They always listened expectantly for the squeak of the last pummelling.

As the weeks went by, however, Belinda saw that the provisions brought with them on the ketch were dwindling. Some of the flour had been wasted by burning the bread, and plainly they hadn't been as frugal with the sugar as their mama would have been. After a time, the potatoes and the dried peas gave out and she remembered her mother had said that, for greens, they could eat the creeper called New Zealand spinach. This creeper with its three-cornered leaf grew in some of the folds around the coast. The children didn't much care for it, declaring it to be a weed, but Belinda said they must eat it if they didn't want to get sick.

"None of you must get sick," she warned, "because there is no one to help you get better."

That made Bobby wail at once that he had a stomach-ache, and Belinda had to send him outside the hut to wail his stomach-ache away alone. But she saw that he ate his spinach and kept the glow of health.

They counted off the days on the calendar that their father had brought with them and hung on the hut wall.

On the square for 14 October, Belinda marked the day of the fatality with her red crayon, and every long day that followed was marked off in black. Long, long days and long, black nights. Sometimes it was hard to believe that there were other people on that coast across the water. There was never any sign of human activity. Sometimes they wondered, if no one ever came, what their end would be.

OCTOBER 1895

Sun		6	13	20 27
Mon		7	14	21 28
Tues	1	8	15 22	29
Wed	2	9	16 23	30
Thurs	3	10	17 24	31
Fri	4	11	18 25	
Sat	5	12	19 26	

Then came the day when their salt meat was finished. If Father and Mother had been here, it would have lasted longer, for Father or Walter would have killed a sheep in between times to eke out the rations. But the children had gone on eating the salt meat until it was finished, partly because they weren't sure that they could kill a sheep.

Weeks now had passed since the tragedy. Not only was their meat exhausted but, because they hadn't known how to be as provident as their parents, their dry supplies were near exhaustion, too. Soon they would only have mutton to live on.

Belinda and Albert discussed the situation.

"Reckon we'll have to kill a sheep, Belinda," Albert said, "skin it, dress it. Gotta eat."

In a few weeks time, in the middle of December, Albert would be ten. Double figures meant growing-up.

"Yes," said Belinda. "Best not to wait until we've used up every scrap of flour . . . best to try to stretch it out a bit. We should have been more careful from the start, but I thought that someone would soon come. Perhaps we should have kept the two fires going."

"Mr Parker *must* come at the end of the year. *You're sure he'll come, Belinda, aren't you?*" He looked hard at Belinda, badly wanting assurance, yet knowing that she had no answer. "An' we'll be all right till then, if we kill a sheep now."

Albert got out his father's butcher's knife. Like Belinda, who had so often watched her mother breadmaking, so Albert had watched his father kill a sheep for the table. He had never done it, but he knew how it should be done. And, since he was seven, he had been helping around the farm.

He and Belinda went out the hut and up the grassy rise to select an animal for slaughter. After a time they manoeuvred an animal into the pen that their father had made. Then Albert grasped his father's knife. His father, not his mother, would have done the killing so now it must be him, not Belinda, who killed this animal for food.

His young face was very set when he entered the pen. Mercifully, he had learnt well from his father, and the job was quick. Then there was the skinning of the animal, the removal of the entrails, the quartering of the beast. It was a long, heavy task for arms that were still thin.

That night they ate roast leg of mutton with the New Zealand spinach.

"Better than salt beef," Albert said, full and relaxed. The meat had tasted good, and there was more hanging in the calico bag from the rafters of the shed. He had been able to do what he had been thinking he might have to do, and rather dreading, all these weeks.

The days were warmer now though the winds still blew, and the black marks were marching across, and up and down, the face of the calendar. Surely someone would come.

They weren't quite so consistent with their fires now. It didn't seem that there was anyone in the world to see their smoke. They began to lose faith in this signalling power. Sometimes they forgot about the fires and let them go out. Then Belinda would feel guilty and set them all collecting driftwood again—though it was getting scarce indeed—and more burnable bits of scrub, and tufts of the yellowing poa grass.

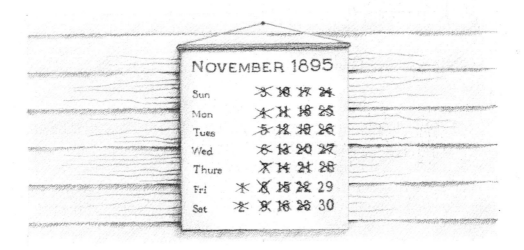

And then on 29 November, Mr James Parker came. He came in his ketch and the children saw the boat coming, bobbing over the white fleece of the waves from the direction of Stanley on the mainland, many kilometres and many turns and twists of the coast away. He was carrying the team of shearers.

He nosed the small craft into the landing-stage and jumped ashore.

"Saw your smoke this morning," he said. "First time I've been this way for a long time. Yer father getting a bit anxious, eh? Run out of provisions or something?"

The children were drawn up on the shingled pebbles looking at him. Looking at him as though he was something strange, a creature almost unknown to them. They stared at him.

"What's wrong?" he cried, knowing at once that all was wrong.

That was when Belinda cried out and ran to him, and then all the children, and each one, in his own way, told what had happened.

"Six weeks! You've been here alone, six weeks!" He was dismayed.

James Parker could scarcely contain his own sorrow. But he gathered the orphans into his ketch and took them across the bouncy uncaring sea to Duck River, to relatives. And when the story was told, they searched Bird Island for Albert Boyes Kay but found no trace.

None of the children was eager to talk of the tragedy. Perhaps because they were pressured so much for detail, and it had been a terrible experience which they didn't want to live over and over again. Even when they were older they didn't speak of it, not even to their own children.

Relatives in the district brought up the six orphans. Five of them grew up to marry and have children of their own, some of whom continued to live in the area of Circular Head. But Belinda, whose determination and inner strength had kept up the spirits and health of her brothers and sisters, never married and died, while still a young woman, from pneumonia.

Sheep still graze on Trefoil. And men still regard the crossing of the rip between the island and the mainland as no less dangerous today than it was in 1895.

Written by Mavis Thorpe Clark
Illustrated by Lisa Herriman

Words to watch for

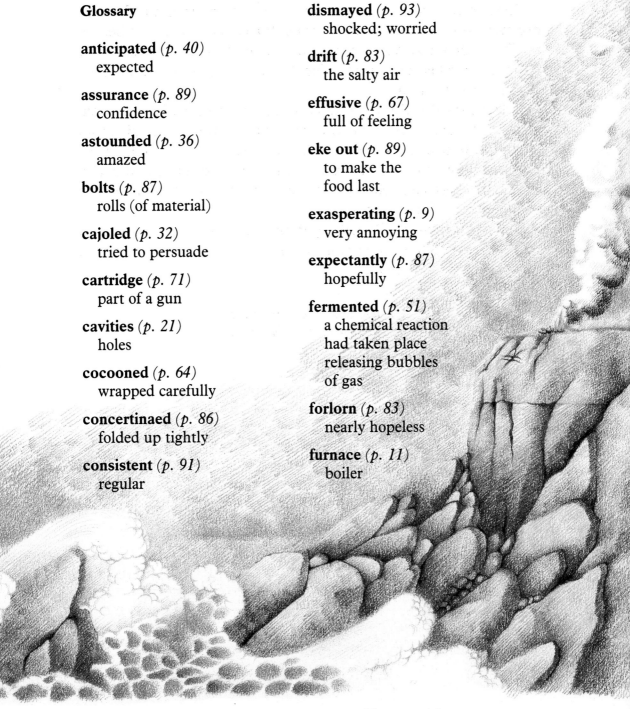

Glossary

anticipated *(p. 40)*
expected

assurance *(p. 89)*
confidence

astounded *(p. 36)*
amazed

bolts *(p. 87)*
rolls (of material)

cajoled *(p. 32)*
tried to persuade

cartridge *(p. 71)*
part of a gun

cavities *(p. 21)*
holes

cocooned *(p. 64)*
wrapped carefully

concertinaed *(p. 86)*
folded up tightly

consistent *(p. 91)*
regular

dismayed *(p. 93)*
shocked; worried

drift *(p. 83)*
the salty air

effusive *(p. 67)*
full of feeling

eke out *(p. 89)*
to make the
food last

exasperating *(p. 9)*
very annoying

expectantly *(p. 87)*
hopefully

fermented *(p. 51)*
a chemical reaction
had taken place
releasing bubbles
of gas

forlorn *(p. 83)*
nearly hopeless

furnace *(p. 11)*
boiler

Glossary continues on
page 96

gawped (*p. 34*)
stared stupidly

groom (*p. 63*)
person who cleans
and looks after
horses

grouching (*p. 87*)
complaining

hushed (*p. 57*)
quiet

indignantly (*p. 31*)
angrily

immigrant (*p. 11*)
a person who
moves to a new
country to live

ketch (*p. 88*)
a two-masted
sailing boat

krill (*p. 83*)
small shrimp-like
creatures

leased (*p. 83*)
paid the owner
money so that he
could use the land

nought (*p. 86*)
nothing

on tenterhooks
(*p. 34*)
in suspense

orthodontist (*p. 13*)
a dentist
concerned with
preventing
irregularities in the
teeth

pleaded (*p. 55*)
asked seriously
and humbly for
something

rip (*p. 94*)
narrow strip of sea

scowling (*p. 60*)
frowning

slaughter (*p. 89*)
killing

tentatively (*p. 35*)
cautiously;
carefully

unleavened (*p.51*)
bread made
without any yeast